★ SELF-DE[

HOW TO PUNCH

PUNCH

UNARMED COMBAT SKILLS THAT WORK

Martin J. Dougherty

THOMAS DUNNE BOOKS
ST. MARTIN'S GRIFFIN ⚘ NEW YORK

THOMAS DUNNE BOOKS
An imprint of St. Martin's Press

Self-Defense: How to Punch.
Copyright © 2013 by Amber Books Ltd. All rights reserved.
For information, address St. Martin's Press, 175 Fifth Avenue,
New York, N.Y. 10010.

www.stmartins.com

Library of Congress Cataloging-in-Publication Data
on file at the Library of Congress

ISBN: 978-1-250-04194-4 (trade paperback)

Editorial and design by
Amber Books Ltd
Bradley's Close
74–77 White Lion Street
London N1 9PF
United Kingdom
www.amberbooks.co.uk

Project Editor: Michael Spilling
Illustrations: Tony Randell

Printed in China

St. Martin's Griffin books may be purchased for educational,
business, or promotional use. For information on bulk purchases,
please contact Macmillan Corporate and Premium Sales Department at
1-800-221-7945 extension 5442 or write specialmarkets@macmillan.com.

First U.S. Edition

10 9 8 7 6 5 4 3 2 1

PUBLISHER'S NOTE
This book is for information purposes only. Readers should be aware of
the legal position in their country of residence before practicing any of the
techniques described in this book. Neither the author or the publisher can
accept responsibility for any loss, injury, or damage caused as a result of
the use of the combat techniques described in this book, nor for any
prosecutions or proceedings brought or instigated against any person
or body that may result from using these techniques.

Contents

Introduction

Punching with a closed fist is not a natural movement. Observations of apes or angry young children suggest that a hammering action with the base of the fists is much more instinctive. It is not surprising, then, that most people who try to punch make a fairly poor job of it.

Executed properly, a punch with the knuckles is an extremely effective means of delivering force and incapacitating an opponent. Whether for sporting or self-defence purposes, the ability to put an opponent down with just one or two blows is one to be valued… although it is only gained through learning to perform the motion correctly and through diligent practice.

Enthusiasm can only go so far in making up for a lack of skill. Big, wild swings are inefficient and tiring, and are easy to avoid for those who know what they are doing. Of course, such 'haymakers', as they are known, are still dangerous if they connect. Anyone throwing a punch should be taken seriously, no matter how poorly it is executed. Even incompetents get lucky sometimes, and someone who throws a barrage of vigorous but inelegant haymakers can easily batter an opponent into submission – assuming that he does not know what to do about it.

Being Effective

In order to punch effectively it is also necessary to be able to move into position for a good solid strike and to deal with attacks coming the other way. Punching is not a matter of using an arm to best effect; a good punch uses the whole body to put weight behind the strike. It is carried into position by crisp, purposeful movement, and again this is a matter of using the whole body effectively.

There are several theories about how to punch most effectively, many of them enshrined in one or more of the martial arts. There are few martial arts that look totally unimpressive when demonstrated by zealous practitioners, so it can be hard to determine which are the most effective. Perhaps it could even be that all of them are right, and that all punching techniques are equally valid?

That, sadly, is not the case. Rather than looking at any given martial art as a whole, it is more useful to look at the punching action as it is used in many arts and to seek common factors. If just one art out of dozens is doing something, then either they have found something wonderful and everyone else is an idiot for not doing it, or more likely there is a

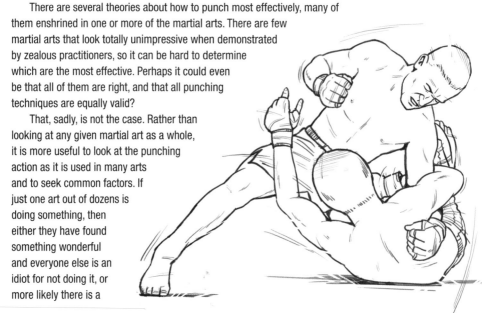

eason for doing it that
ay that is specific to
at art – and therefore
ot necessarily a
niversal truth.

The term 'martial
rt' has connotations
f fighting or perhaps
ilitary use, and it is
easonable to say that all
martial arts started out as fighting
ystems. However, over time many
ave evolved into something else.
n art that is no longer geared
 fighting will probably still be
 worthy athletic endeavour
nd will surely require great
kill, but lessons about how
 fight cannot be drawn
om martial arts that are
o longer geared towards
ghting.

Combat Sports

It is to combat sports rather than martial arts that we must turn to see what works. Some martial arts are of course also combat sports, although some of them are pure grappling arts and have nothing to teach about striking. Those that remain can teach valuable lessons, and they have a surprising amount in common.

Mixed martial arts (MMA), boxing, many styles of kickboxing, muay thai and similar systems have retained their combat focus through full-contact competition. If a particular way of striking is effective against a conditioned and trained athlete who is expecting to be hit and willing to take a few in order to win, then we can be assured that it works, and works well.

This, really, is the only test that counts. If a way of striking stands the test of combat then we can believe in it, and, short of going out picking fights with random strangers, the only way to pressure-test a system is to compete or engage in full-contact sparring with an opponent who is determined to win the bout.

Comparing the striking styles that have proven effective in competition, it is obvious that boxing-style punches are extremely potent. In mixed martial arts competition, where athletes are free to choose how they strike, we do not see karate or kung fu style punches very often.

What we do see is a fairly generic system that has shown its effectiveness in a vast number of sporting bouts and 'real world' encounters too. Straight and hooked punches delivered with good weight transference from a tight guard, slips and deflections on the defensive, and adherence to certain principles that seem to be common to all the effective punching arts.

In short, there is much to be learned from various martial arts, but we must not forget that a punch is an attempt to deliver force with the intent of hurting someone. However amazing a method looks, if it fails to hit hard and put the other guy down then something important is missing.

Striking with the Hands
The hands are an effective striking tool if used properly. The key is to remember that the hand is only a striking surface — it is the part that makes contact with the target, but force is transmitted from your body through the hand rather than coming from the hand.

Aligning the Hand
There are various theories about which knuckles should impact first but what tends to happen is that the middle two often make contact whatever the intention may have been. The hand should be aligned so that force is transmitted straight up the wrist and forearm; punching styles that use a misaligned wrist are no good for hitting anything but air.

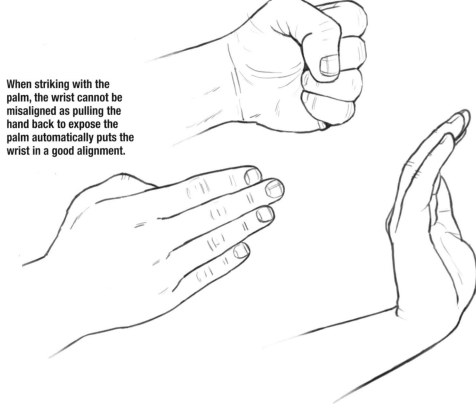

When striking with the palm, the wrist cannot be misaligned as pulling the hand back to expose the palm automatically puts the wrist in a good alignment.

Avoiding Damage
The hand has many small bones that can be fractured by impact, and digits (fingers and thumbs) can be dislocated if they catch on something while executing a punch. The wrist is also vulnerable, as it can collapse if not properly aligned, which will at least weaken the blow and can cause damage to the soft tissues of the wrist.

Making a Fist

A good, tight fist is important when striking with the hand. The thumb should be curled and resting across the first knuckles of the top fingers, but not wrapped in so tight as to be uncomfortable. It must never stick out where it can catch on anything, which can sometimes happen when a puncher is used to wearing bag gloves to train and has become lazy about forming a fist properly.

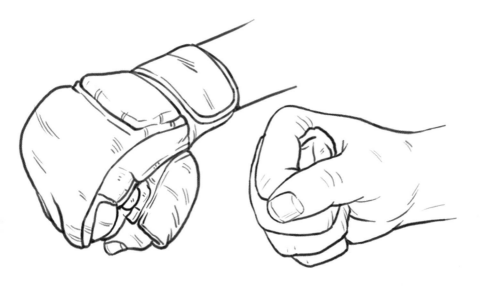

Striking with a Fist

The hand can be supported by holding an object in the palm when making a fist. Many styles of bag gloves have a bar in the palm for this purpose, and something as simple as holding a handkerchief in the hand can help form the fist properly. If there is nothing available to support the hand, balling it up tight works well – this also helps align the wrist properly and forms the muscles of the forearm to resist any chance of wrist collapse.

Palm Strikes and Cupped Hand Strikes

A palm strike is not a punch but uses the same mechanics and is every bit as effective in delivering force. Palm strikes can be substituted for punches to the head when you are not wearing gloves to protect your fist. Your hand and wrist are much less likely to be damaged this way.

Striking with the Palm

Palm strikes are delivered with the fleshy pad at the base of the palm. Rather than being balled into a fist, the hand is pulled back and the digits only slightly curled to keep them out of the way. The blow is executed with the same mechanics as a punch.

Strike with the fleshy pad at the base of the palm.

Drive it straight in with body weight – and conviction – behind it.

Think of the palm strike as a battering ram smashing through your opponent.

The Cupped-Hand Strike

The cupped-hand strike or 'powerslap' is similar to a hook punch, just like a palm heel strike is similar to a straight punch. The target is a point just below the ear, at the back end of the jawbone. The striking point is the fleshy base of your palm, opposite the thumb.

Strike with the base of the palm. Cupping the hand increases the amount of protection this fleshy area gives to the bones of the striking hand.

The target is the side of the head at the back of the jawbone. Hitting here transmits shock straight to the base of the brain and can cause a quick knockout.

Wave Motion

The cupped-hand strike should travel upwards as well as inwards towards the target. It moves in a wave-like motion, up and in. After impact the strike would carry on moving and arc back down if the opponent's head had not stopped it.

Palm Strikes for Self-Defence

Striking with the palm is illegal in many forms of competition, but if forced to take your punching skills out of the sporting arena and into a 'street' confrontation, palm strikes let you use your punching skills without fear of damaging yourself. That said, it is not 'incorrect' to punch without hand protection. If your safety is threatened and you have to strike someone to protect yourself, then success is what matters.

Targets and Effects

Some parts of the body, such as the eyes and genitals, are very vulnerable – even a weak blow can cause enough pain to put someone out of a fight. However, the operative word is 'can'. Such blows are usually illegal in competition, and relying on a single sniper-like shot to end a street fight can be a problem if it does not work.

Body Shots

It has wisely been said that 'head shots hurt. Body shots hurt the whole fight'. While a body blow is not likely to end a fight in the same way that a knockout shot to the head might, it can weaken the opponent and allow him to be finished off, and a body blow that connects just right can wind someone so badly that they cannot continue.

Most fighting stances guard the head as a primary target and the body as a secondary concern. A headshot can put you down instantly; a body blow is less likely to cause immediate defeat.

'Cheap shots' to the genitals, eyes and throat can be effective for self-defence, especially since they require only a little force. There is, however, no guarantee that the opponent will be stopped.

Many ill-aimed blows strike tougher or less vital areas of the body and head, landing on arms or shoulders, or parts of the face that can suffer damage without resulting in a knockout. A blow to the cheekbone might cause a black eye, but it is unlikely to result in a knockout.

Headshots

The head is, for the most part, hard and well protected. However, blows that rock the head front to back or whip it around from side to side can cause 'brain shake' that leads to unconsciousness or disorientation. Most untrained fighters will instinctively attack the head since it is the seat of consciousness.

Where Not to Hit

It is fairly pointless to punch the limbs. It is possible to give an opponent a 'dead leg' by striking the leg muscles but this is a hugely inefficient way of winning a fight and lays the puncher open to being hit in the head as he is reaching in. Thus most blows are directed at the body and head. However, the upper chest is not worth punching, as it is too well protected by muscle and ribs; the same goes for most of the back.

Striking the Head

The primary target for punching at the front of the head is the 'button', the very front of the jaw directly below the mouth. Hooked punches or strikes from the side are also best aimed at the front part of the jaw. The jaw itself is extremely hard, which is a mixed blessing – on the one hand it transmits force to the rest of the head very well; on the other a bad contact can result in a broken hand.

Blows to the Face

Blows to the nose and cheekbones can break them, although this is less likely with gloves on, but most ill-aimed strikes to the head are unlikely to cause much harm. They are, however, painful, and most people have an instinctive fear of being attacked in the face that can cause a fighter to panic or give up.

The One You Don't See

The rule of thumb is that 'it's the one you don't see that drops you'. Caught unawares by a blow (i.e. with the neck muscles relaxed) you will suffer much greater forces on the brain and might well be dropped by a shot that you would otherwise have coped with.

Mixing It Up

An unskilled opponent will tend to flail away with heavy swings at the head, which are easy to see coming. A skilled fighter will switch between body and headshots, straight and hooked blows, and will probably position himself for a more solid contact.

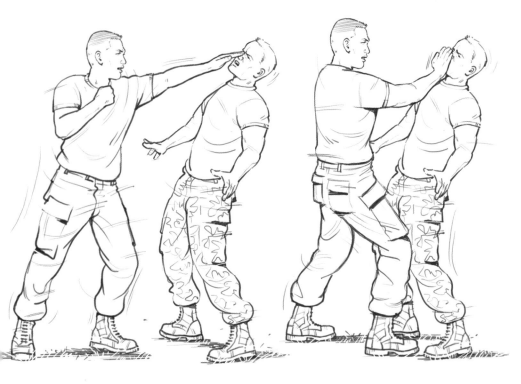

Different kinds of strikes are effective against the head, including palm hits to the chin and straight-fingered strikes to the eyes.

The Head is Surprisingly Resilient

In the course of a long bout, a boxer's head can take a fearful battering without causing unconsciousness. One reason for this is that if a fighter can see a blow coming then he can 'ride' it. He may be able to move so that the contact is mitigated somewhat, and his neck muscles can cushion the whipping action of his head.

Striking the Body
Body blows should be travelling horizontally or upwards, and should be driven in deep.

Primary Targets – Front
A blow to the sternum is very painful, and just below it is the solar plexus, which is perhaps the ideal spot to strike with a body blow. Anywhere along the horizontal line from the solar plexus is a good target as it will shock the diaphragm and make breathing much more difficult.

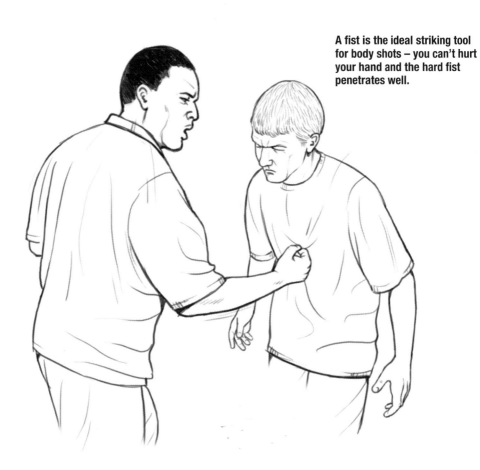

A fist is the ideal striking tool for body shots – you can't hurt your hand and the hard fist penetrates well.

Primary Targets – Sides and Rear
From the sides and rear, the diaphragm line (and just below it) and the kidney area are productive targets, and a strike to the side of the rib cage, close under the armpit, is also often effective.

Strike Upwards...

Most body shots are delivered just below the rib cage to attack the internal organs and diaphragm. Striking upwards just under the bottom of the ribs delivers force to the internal organs, which is extremely painful and can drop an opponent in his tracks.

A body shot may not cause a knockout, but it will make it difficult for the opponent to move, fight or chase you, and it can open him up for a finishing blow to the head.

...Not Downwards

A blow to the same spot that was travelling downwards would have much less effect due to the way the body is constructed. Blows to the front of the abdomen are less effective, especially against conditioned opponents who have well-developed abdominal muscles.

Stance, Guard and Movement

An orthodox fighter will stand weak-side-forward. That is, if he is right handed he will have his left side closer to the opponent. The body is angled at around 45 degrees with the lead shoulder slightly raised to protect the jaw. The chin is down and tucked in, eyes rolled up a little so that the brow protects the face.

The Boxer's Guard

The generic 'boxer's guard' is used by many martial arts and self-defence systems. It offers a good combination of a solid base and quick mobility, tight defence and a good platform for launching attacks.

Hands

Hands should be roughly at chin height, curled fairly loosely unless a punch is being delivered, and elbows down to protect the ribs. At risk of being overly simplistic, the lead hand is for speed to make openings and the strong hand is for doing damage.

One of the best ways not to get hit is not to be there. Constant movement makes you a difficult target.

Feet

The feet are turned in as far as necessary to make this position fairly comfortable. The front foot usually turns in less than the back one. Weight is on the balls of the feet and more or less evenly distributed between them.

Movement

Movement can be used to open and close the distance between you and the opponent, ideally causing his attacks to fall just a little short and putting you in a good place to counterattack. The only good reason to be in front of an opponent and at the right distance to hit or be hit is because you intend to attack. If you are not intending to attack imminently, keep your distance and allow yourself a little more time to react if he launches punches of his own.

You can only hit what you can reach; move in to striking distance when you want to attack and stay out when you do not.

The Shuffle

Movement uses a shuffling action. This is accomplished by pushing with whichever foot is furthest from the direction you want to move in and stepping a short distance with the other. Big strides are not a good idea, and the feet should not cross.

Sidestep and Pivot

It is possible to move in any direction using the shuffle – straight forward and back, to the sides or diagonally, or to circle the opponent by stepping diagonally and pivoting the body to keep the opponent directly in front. Your weapons, so to speak, shoot directly forwards so it is important not to allow an opponent to circle around to the side. If he can get to a position where his weapons are aimed at you and yours are pointing into empty air, he gains a significant advantage. This can be offset by simply turning to face him, of course.

17

Hitting Hard

There is no point in hitting someone gently. If it is necessary to hit then blows should land hard and have an effect. Light, fast jabs are often used for tactical purposes rather than to put an opponent down, but all the same it is important that they are not a token gesture – even a quick jab should hurt the opponent enough to be worth throwing.

An opponent who realizes that your shots are not hurting him will walk through them and demolish you. Thus any strike should not be a token gesture – it should hit hard and it should hurt.

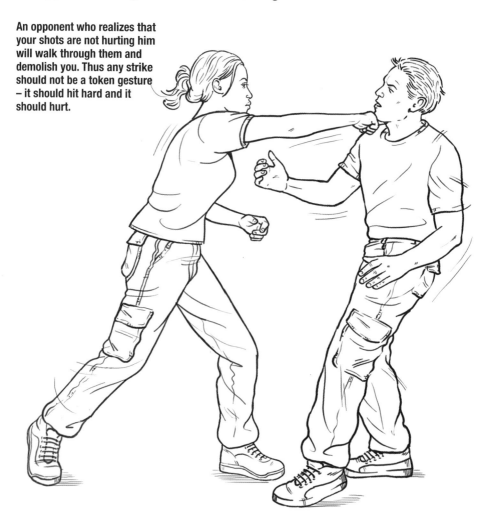

Driving into the Target

A good punch travels fast and accurately, and hits hard. It is driven into the target rather than landing on the surface. A good rule of thumb is to try to punch right through the target, or at least several inches into it. Remember that the same amount of force delivered slowly will push the target around rather than damaging it – speed is vital in maximizing the impact of a blow.

Body weight can be transferred to a blow by a 'wading in' motion or heavy, launching steps. While crude, these methods do work but they are slow and can be 'pushy' rather than damaging.

ntrained or poorly trained
ghters often try to generate
ower with big motions, taking
vild swings or winding up
traight punches by retracting
ne arm first.

Weight Transference

Most people try to punch with just their arms, but for a powerful strike you need to get your weight behind the shot. Good body mechanics will drive the shot into the target and get a result far beyond what just swinging an arm could achieve.

Breathing

Breathing is vital to your continued existence, and more immediately to your ability to fight. There is a strange tendency to hold your breath as you do something strenuous; in a fight this is disastrous. A fight uses up tremendous amounts of oxygen, and a fighter who gets out of breath will be easily defeated by one who still has a little gas in the tank.

Never become so focussed on what you are doing that you forget to breathe. It can and will happen, and it can cost you the fight.

Keep Breathing!

Breathing out on a strike forces the body to breathe in afterwards, which ensures that more air is drawn in to fuel all the other shots that you might still have to launch. Disciplined breathing means you will be able to move offensively and defensively, and to throw harder punches for longer.

Breathe Out on Every Strike

You should breathe out as you make every strike. It does not matter about making the right noises when you breathe so long as you move a sufficient quantity of air in and out. You can grunt, snarl or even yodel if you like, but just keep that air moving.

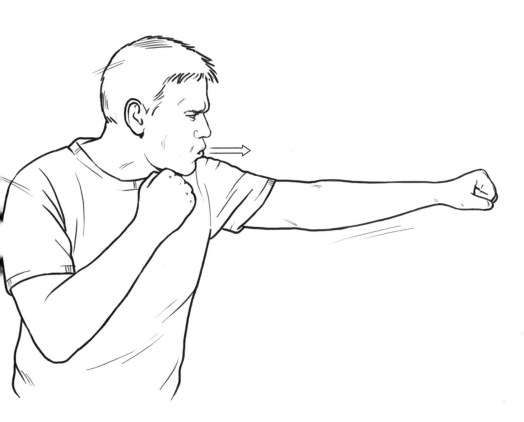

Breathe for Attack and Defence

Breathing out on every strike increases the power of your shots. It tightens up your torso, which allows a harder strike to be launched and may reduce the effects of being hit on the body.

Straight Punches

A straight strike is faster than a hooked one, enabling you to beat the opponent to the punch. It is important not to draw the hand back before throwing the strike. Instead, the hand comes forward from your guard position, directly at the target.

Power Generation

Power is generated by weight transference; punching with just the arm is likely to be ineffective. A slight step forward as the lead hand strikes adds much to the impact, while a strong-hand blow comes all the way from the toes of the back foot. The hip and shoulder are pushed forward as the arm comes out to strike, delivering a maximized blow with the whole of the body behind it.

A straight strike should be just that – straight. It does not travel in a curve and the hand is not retracted before throwing the shot.

A good guard position holds your hands in the right place to throw a straight punch; moving them elsewhere gives away your intentions, wastes time and may leave you open to a counterpunch as you wind-up.

Good Posture

Do not lean into a strike. Maintain a good body structure. This allows you to throw more strikes, to defend or to move away to avoid retaliation.

The Lead Straight

A lead straight is more committed than a jab and is intended to cause real harm. It is thrown with slight forward movement to add some weight to the blow, and it can stun an opponent long enough for a fight-finishing strong-hand shot. There is no point in throwing a lead straight unless you have a clear target. If the opportunity is a bit low-percentage then a lighter, less committed jab will suffice.

Avoid dropping the hand after a jab or any other strike; pull it straight back instead.

The Jab

The jab is a fast, light strike thrown mainly to gauge the distance and keep the opponent guessing. In a sporting match, many lead-hand punches will be light jabs that conserve energy while not letting the opponent have his own way. It is worth getting as much as possible out of the jab if it can be done without wasting too much energy, but jabs should not be heavily committed.

Angle

On a straight punch, the hand will naturally find itself somewhere between horizontal and a 45-degree angle. Forcing it to a vertical or fully horizontal position increases tension in the arm and shortens reach – neither is desirable.

The Cross

The cross is a strong-hand punch intended to do some serious harm to the opponent. Like the jab, it is thrown from your guard position without a big wind-up, and it travels in a straight line. A cross comes diagonally across the body and will usually impact the opponent's chin.

Reaching the Opponent

In order to reach the opponent, the whole side of the body needs to be brought forward. This is not a problem, however, as it is done anyway to generate power. As with other punches, the cross travels fast and light with a relaxed arm and is then driven deep into the target.

Combinations

Crosses are rarely thrown in isolation, and normally follow a jab or lead straight. The lead-hand shot covers the fighter's approach into striking distance, finds the range and hopefully opens the opponent up, at which point the cross is delivered. If the lead hand does not find the target then the cross is not thrown, saving energy.

The cross is a potentially fight-ending blow, but you have to get into position to launch it. Lead-hand strikes are often used to set up the cross.

Most fighters will circle away from their opponent's strong hand – which usually means they move to the right. Moving the other way risks walking onto a powerful punch.

Hooked Punches

As the name suggests, hooked strikes follow a curved path. This takes longer to reach the target than a straight shot, which means that a straight punch launched at the same time your opponent throws a hook will get there first and possibly serve as an entirely effective defence. Untrained fighters will often unleash a barrage of big swinging punches that can cause serious damage but are easy to see coming and avoid. A good hooked strike is tight, disciplined and requires practice to perfect.

Generating Power

Rather than just swinging the arm, the fighter generates power by turning his body into the strike, using good body mechanics to create a solid frame that supports the strike.

Hooks are short-range shots, and they should only be thrown from close in. If you have to reach for the opponent with your hook you're too far away for it to be fully effective.

Tight Arc

Hooked punches are thrown in a tight arc. For best effect the punch should not be moving away from you when it lands. It should instead be travelling across your front or even coming back towards you a little.

Setting Up a Hook

A skilled puncher will normally move forward as he throws his straight shots, then get in close and deliver hooks to the body and head. Switching from straight to hooked shots can defeat the opponent's defence or deliver a fight-ending blow.

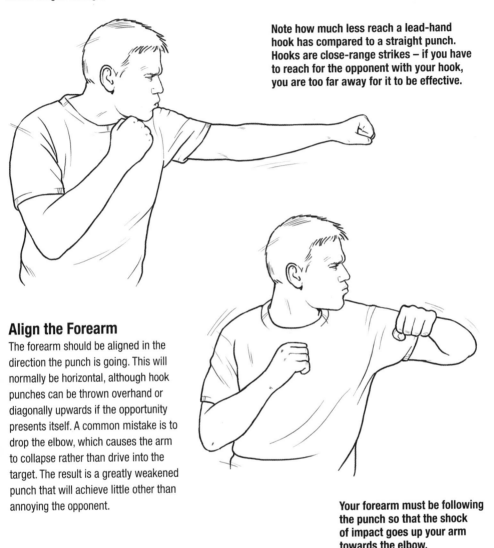

Note how much less reach a lead-hand hook has compared to a straight punch. Hooks are close-range strikes – if you have to reach for the opponent with your hook, you are too far away for it to be effective.

Align the Forearm

The forearm should be aligned in the direction the punch is going. This will normally be horizontal, although hook punches can be thrown overhand or diagonally upwards if the opportunity presents itself. A common mistake is to drop the elbow, which causes the arm to collapse rather than drive into the target. The result is a greatly weakened punch that will achieve little other than annoying the opponent.

Your forearm must be following the punch so that the shock of impact goes up your arm towards the elbow.

Do Not Overextend

Hurling your entire body into a strike will compromise your balance even if you land your blow, and it may actually rob your punch of force. Good body structure must be maintained throughout – a twisted, awkward stance cannot generate suitable force and will also make it difficult to throw fast or accurate punches.

Hook Punch

A strong-hand hook punch is normally just referred to as a hook. It travels along a similar path to a lead-hand hook but, obviously, in the opposite direction. A good hook is tight and powerful and is driven into the target by allowing the hip and shoulder to come forward and pivot in the direction of the blow. The feet also have to pivot, with the back foot moving around more than the front.

Most hooks go into the side of the target, but if you are off to the side it can be possible to slam a hook into the frontal diaphragm area, which can seriously impair an opponent's ability to fight.

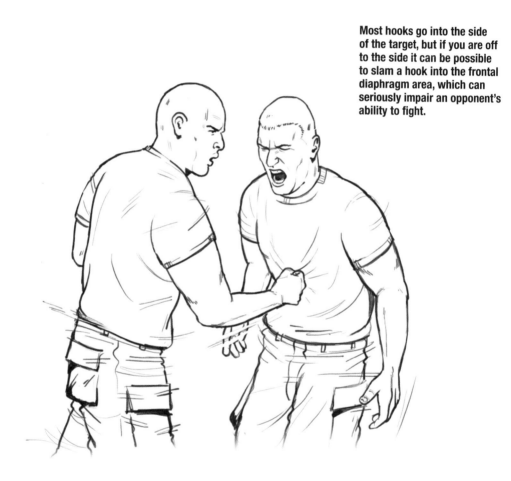

Body Hooks

Similar comments apply to body hooks, which are normally thrown into the kidney area with a vertical fist. It is harder to twist into a body hook than one delivered to the head, but a sharp twisting motion of the body is still necessary in order to deliver force. Often the shoulder is pushed forward over the hook; this applies with body hooks thrown with either the lead or the strong hand.

Using the Body Hook

Body hooks will often draw the opponent's guard down as he pulls his elbows in to protect his flanks. This will open up the head much of the time. Even if it is not possible to get a good head shot in, body blows will impair an opponent's breathing and reduce his ability to fight even if they do not cause him to simply give up.

The typical guard position covers the straight lines of attack but can be avoided by going around it. If the opponent shifts to a wide guard to prevent this, a straight shot may get through.

The Shovel Hook

The shovel hook, or body punch, is hooked vertically rather than horizontally. It is used to deliver a direct blow into the torso, usually to the front up under the ribs. If you can move around to the side, a shovel hook to the liver or kidney area can be very effective.

Lead-Hand Hook

The lead-hand hook is a sharp and fast movement that can come in over the opponent's guard and often takes him by surprise. A lead-hand hook can be thrown from a guard position or can be used to follow up a jab. In that case, the jabbing hand is partially retracted and the elbow raised to follow the line of the punch.

Body Alignment

The lead hook is driven into the target by a twisting motion of the body, pushing the left shoulder forward and dragging the punch into the target using the pectoral muscles. The whole body needs to turn into the punch, with the front foot pivoting (on the ball of the foot) to point in the direction of the blow as if crushing a cockroach or putting out a cigarette underfoot. A hook thrown with the foot pointing forward will be very weak.

The lead-hand hook requires a lot of practice to perform well, but it is a potent strike and well worth the effort.

Lead-Lead Hook Combination

Most fighters punch with alternate hands, left-right-left-right, so a jab-lead hook combination can catch out an opponent who expects a right-hand punch to follow a jab. It is necessary to close in behind the jab, of course, or the punch will not land. Correct body mechanics are also vital as the lead hook does not have much time to gather momentum and thus needs to be delivered well if it is to work at all.

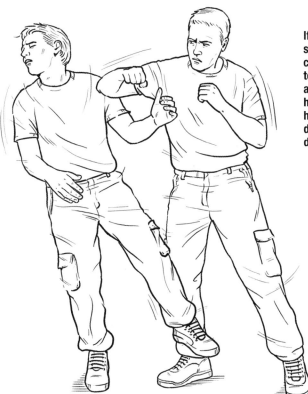

If the opponent is rattled by a solid lead straight, a lead hook can be an excellent finishing tool. It arrives too quickly after the first blow to allow him to recover and snaps the head around in a different direction, causing even more disorientation.

The Uppercut

The uppercut is in many ways similar to the shovel hook. It travels up the centre of the body, under the chin, and is delivered with a similar motion to the shovel hook, but curves upward rather than being driven forward. It is a short-range strike that can result in an instant knockout as it hits home under the chin and snaps the head back.

Delivering an Uppercut

The uppercut is delivered with a slight crouch and given additional force by the fighter's back and legs as he comes out of his crouch at the moment of impact.

If you can send the opponent reeling back with an uppercut, it is very hard to stop the process and you should gain the opportunity to land several more blows.

he uppercut can be delivered with either the ead or strong hand, although many fighters ind the strong hand to be more accessible due o their body position.

ollowing Up

t the very least, an uppercut will break the pponent's body structure as his head goes back; may make him stumble backwards or at least pen him up to other blows. If he does stumble ack, his guard will usually open up as he tries o regain his balance, allowing you to step in nd deliver a straight right to the head that will ccelerate his rearward progress.

Hammerfists

The hammerfist is an alternative to many hooked strikes. It uses the base of the fist as a striking surface. A tight fist bunches up the flesh of the palm heel and creates a striking surface that protects the hand but still delivers a lot of force.

Hammerfists are an instinctive motion, but do need to be aimed for maximum effect. Battering away at the opponent's chest and shoulders will not defeat him, but a hammerfist to the head might.

Inward Hammerfists

Inward hammerfists follow a similar path to hook punches, or can be delivered downwards with a hammering action. 'Cycling hammerfists' are a good follow-up to an initial strike, delivering a series of inward blows.

The hammerfist is an extremely
powerful striking tool, allowing
you to hit a hard target without
damaging the hand.

Outward Hammerfists

The outward hammerfist is delivered by drawing your arm across your body and then driving the base of
your palm at the target. The motion is sharp and hard, and although less powerful than an inward blow it
can be used to make space or to open up an opponent.

Movement: the Best Defence

A fighter who is static allows his opponent to aim carefully and attack at a moment of his choosing, with an excellent chance of hitting. His own attacks will also be ineffective, since his opponent will see him starting to move. The human eye is very good at noticing a previously stationary object that starts to move, but may not recognize a change in the way that an already moving object behaves.

A fighter who moves well looks like he knows what he is doing. That can unnerve an opponent who may doubt his ability to win the fight.

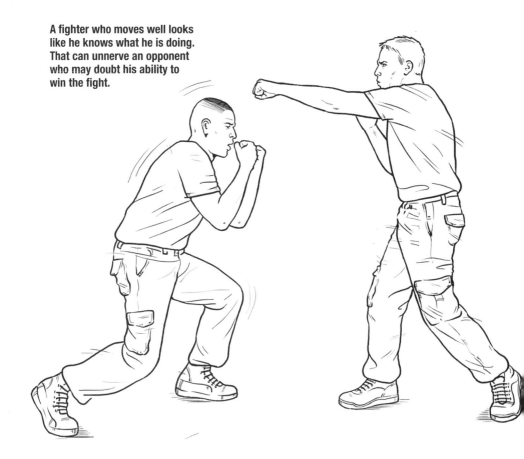

Use Time and Distance

Any blow takes time to travel from start point to target, plus whatever 'internal time' is required to make the decision to strike and to decide how best to do it, to set up the strike and to get into position. If you are moving unpredictably, the opponent may decide not to throw his punch at all – if the chances of hitting seem poor then there may be no point. Even if he does attack he may well miss.

Controlled Movement

Defensive movement does not mean leaping about all over the place. It means small movements of the head and hands accompanied by circling, opening and closing the range, and changes in speed and direction. This should be habitual, especially head movement, so that you do not stop evading when you become tired.

Movement is both offensive and defensive – it puts you where you need to be in order to attack, and denies the opponent opportunities to hit you.

Active Defence

In addition to moving around you should throw fast jabs whenever you are in range. This forces an opponent to deal with the strike, preventing him from attacking, and disguises your intentions to attack with a fully committed strike.

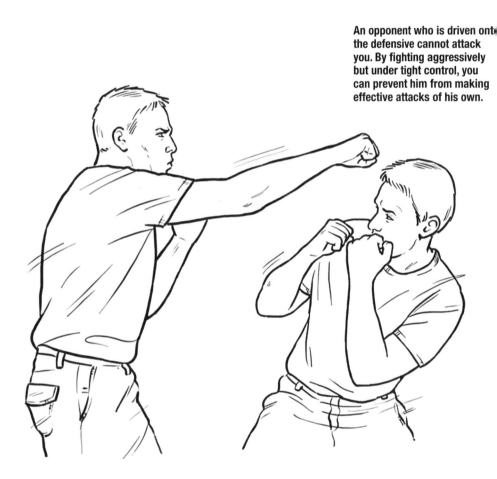

An opponent who is driven onto the defensive cannot attack you. By fighting aggressively but under tight control, you can prevent him from making effective attacks of his own.

Just a Threat Will Do

If an opponent thinks he can simply walk up and hit you, then he will pick his moment and do it. A good guard and your obvious readiness to strike can be enough to defeat many attacks – your opponent may decide that he cannot attack you because you will strike him as he tries.

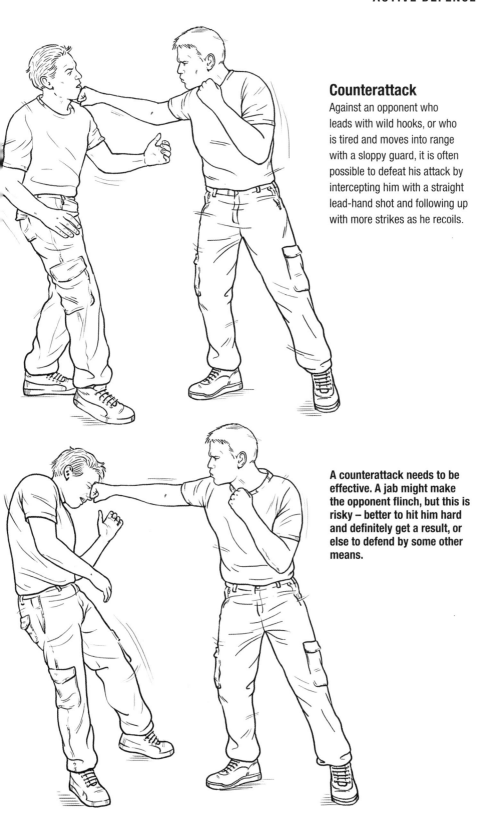

Counterattack

Against an opponent who leads with wild hooks, or who is tired and moves into range with a sloppy guard, it is often possible to defeat his attack by intercepting him with a straight lead-hand shot and following up with more strikes as he recoils.

A counterattack needs to be effective. A jab might make the opponent flinch, but this is risky – better to hit him hard and definitely get a result, or else to defend by some other means.

Cover Defence

Covers are the last line of defence, although using them by no means indicates that you are losing. You may have to cover and ride out a bad situation then get back in the fight once the opponent has expended his burst of energy. Landing powerful shots requires an enormous expenditure of effort, and few fighters can throw more than a few full-power shots in succession before they weaken. If you can survive this, you can come back.

Vertical Cover

A vertical two-handed cover works well against a direct shot from the front, although it does stop you from seeing what the opponent is doing. Keep the elbows tight together to prevent the blow from driving between the arms and keep them close to your body. Tuck the head in behind your vertical forearms, presenting your brow to anything that comes through the cover.

Cover defences are best accompanied by moving forward, shortening and weakening the opponent's strike.

Straight Punch Defence

Bring your hands and forearms up sharply across the body to deflect a straight punch while moving the upper body back to reduce the impact of the blow.

Move and Cover

Standing still to receive a blow is not the best option, although it may be the only one. If possible, weaken the strike by moving inside its arc or away from it, but always ensure that if you receive a blow, your body structure is good. If you are off balance from trying to scramble away from a blow, you may be worse off than if you had simply braced to receive it.

Sometimes there are no better options than covering the target and riding the blow. However, you must get back into the fight – folding up and passively covering only prolongs the beating.

Cross-Guard

The cross-guard covers the same sort of blow as well as many hooks, although it does leave the ribs exposed to an opponent who decides to strike there instead. The cross-guard uses diagonal forearms, parallel to one another, one hand pointing at the opposite armpit and the other above the opposite elbow. A small gap between the arms allows you to peer through and see what the opponent is trying to do next.

Deflecting a Punch

It is possible to deflect shots before they land. This requires an ability to 'read' an opponent's intentions to some extent – a punch that comes as a surprise will be impossible to deflect in time. Deflection is not the same thing as 'blocking' – blocking opposes force with force, which is not always the best option.

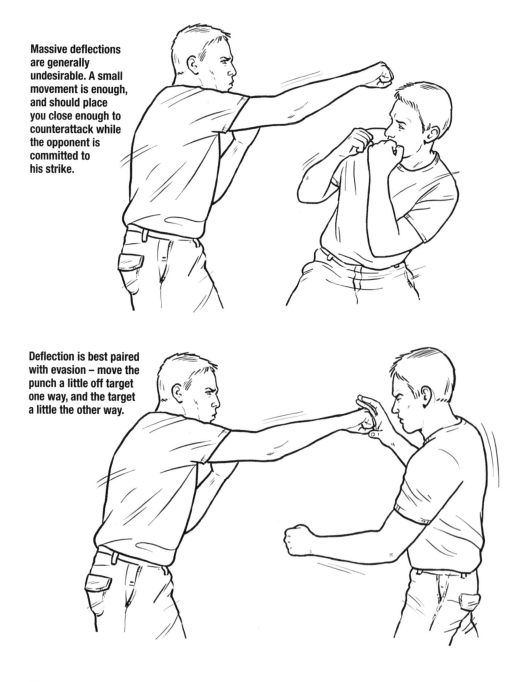

Massive deflections are generally undesirable. A small movement is enough, and should place you close enough to counterattack while the opponent is committed to his strike.

Deflection is best paired with evasion – move the punch a little off target one way, and the target a little the other way.

Deflect, Don't Block

Straight punches can be 'pawed down' or batted to the side with a small movement of the arm – usually the lead arm. Hooks are more difficult to defend against in this manner but can sometimes be deflected by pushing into the crook of the opponent's arm. All that is necessary is to make the punch miss, which does not necessarily equate to stopping it dead.

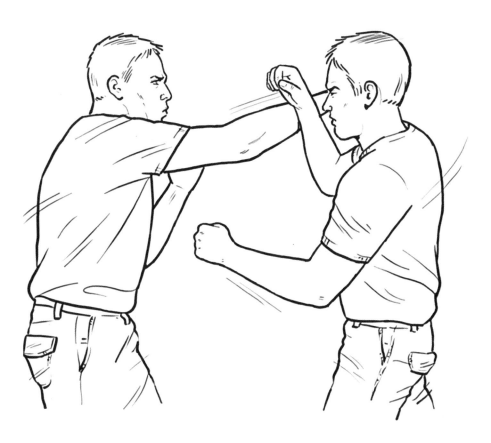

Deflection and Evasion

Deflections are often accompanied by a measure of evasion. It is possible to defeat a punch by swaying back, increasing the range just enough to make it fall short, or by slipping it. This means moving the head to the side just enough that the punch misses. Both are often accompanied by either 'catching' the punch on a defensive hand or 'kissing' it with a small movement of the hand to ensure that it really does go past.

Bob and Weave

It possible to duck under a hook punch to the head. A duck should not be a bend from the waist, resulting in you looking at the floor. It is a crouch, with your eyes still pointing forward, and it's usually accompanied by your hands coming up to cover the head – just in case.

In order to have time to bob-weave it is necessary to 'read' the opponent's intentions. Many fighters will 'telegraph' their intentions with a big wind-up, making their wild swings easier to evade.

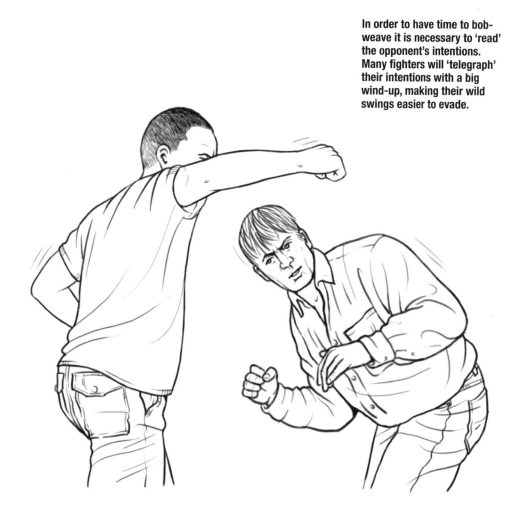

Bob-Weave is Better

A bob-weave is more efficient than ducking. During the ducking movement you move forward and towards the punch, passing under it, and pop back up close to the opponent ready to strike him before he recovers from his own failed blow.

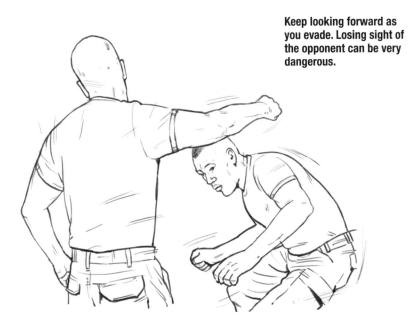

Keep looking forward as
you evade. Losing sight of
the opponent can be very
dangerous.

Countering the Attack

It is possible to strike the opponent's body during the bob-weave movement, or you can pop back up and then unload on him. Some fighters prefer to move back to a position directly in front of the opponent after this defence. Others take advantage of the 'outside' position to attack the opponent from an angle where he cannot easily strike back.

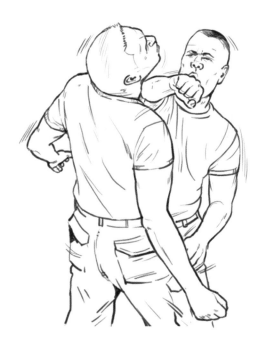

Counterattacking

Counterpunching is something of an art, and requires practice to be effective. The essence of counterpunching is to evade or deflect the opponent's blow and land one of your own. It is also possible to stop his attack by hitting faster or as he prepares his attack, or in such a way that his blow becomes ineffective.

Timing is the Key

A well-timed counterattack can stop an opponent from throwing his own strike. It is essential to beat him to the punch and hit him hard enough, so that whatever he is trying to do is disrupted. You should move immediately after striking, just in case he was not entirely stopped.

Counterpunch Hook Defence

An effective defence against a long hook is to throw a straight counterpunch on the same side. Thus if the opponent launches a long right hook (or a sloppy, partially-hooked straight shot) you can both attack and defend at the same time with a straight left. Keep your head tucked in and your arm high – in this case it helps to roll the hand over so that the thumb end is pointing at a downward angle. This sort of counterpunching defence requires a lot of skill and good timing, however, and is not something to be attempted by beginners.

After hitting, circle to your right
away from your opponent's
strong hand and out of the way
of any wild punch he might
throw in response to your blow.

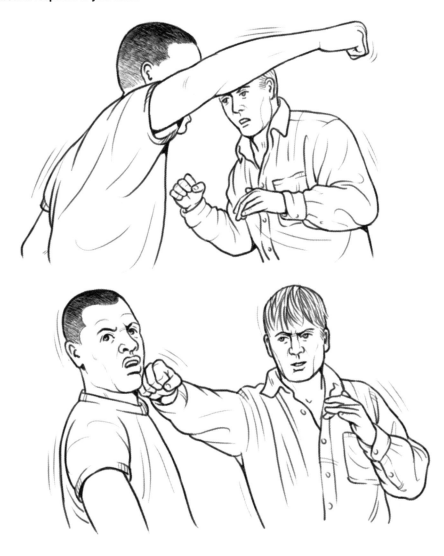

You should now be well
positioned to hit again, opening
up the opponent for a follow-up
as he staggers. If he does not,
the process of move-hit-move
can be continued until you land
a decisive blow.

Final Notes

Ultimately, if you want to learn to punch effectively you need to try it under live conditions. This means sparring with at least a little contact. Stopping as soon as a hit is landed (as is done in martial arts 'points' competitions) is counterproductive. You need to learn to deal with the real fight environment, where several blows may be needed to stop an opponent and making a mistake forces you to deal with quite a few coming the other way. Resetting after a single hit does not replicate this situation.

Sparring is a useful way to practice your skills, but only if it is approached properly. Sparring 'with' a partner is more useful than sparring 'against' an opponent most of the time. If both fighters are trying to hurt one another and win, then it is difficult to work on technique or iron out faults. Most sparring should be light and technical, and often focussed on developing a particular skill. The occasional heavy bout serves to build fighting spirit and to teach how to function under pressure.

As with any fight training, sparring should be approached sensibly and should be supervised by properly qualified people. Protective equipment is necessary – gloves and gumshields at the very least. Most of all, sparring should be seen as part of the learning experience, not 'the fun bit'. Far too many people want to spar too much, too soon and too hard. Sparring is where you try out your skills, and then it's back to the drills and the technical training to improve some more.

Glossary

Combinations: Blows are rarely thrown in isolation. The cross punch, for example, normally follows a jab or straight punch, while a hooked punch may follow a lead straight.

Cross guard: The forearms are held diagonally in front of the face, parallel to one another, to stop the opponent landing blows to the head.

Cross punch: Thrown diagonally from across the body, the cross is a powerful blow intended to do serious harm to an opponent.

Hammerfists: This is a blow with the base of the fist, following an inward, outward or downward curving path. A tight fist is better protected in this position against damage than when striking with the knuckles.

Haymaker: A wild, swinging punch. Untrained fighters generally throw haymakers, which are relatively easy to defend against but dangerous if they land.

Hooked punch: Hooked punches can be thrown with the lead or rear hand, and strike with the knuckles of a closed fist. The wild haymaker is essentially a poorly executed hook targeted at the head.

Jab: A quick strike designed to gauge distance. Can be used to keep an opponent at bay and keep them guessing.

Straight punch: Straight punches with the knuckles of a closed fist include the jab, which is a fast, light strike used mainly in boxing and similar competitions; the lead straight, which is similar but lands with much more force; and the cross, which is a very powerful blow delivered from the rear hand.

Uppercut: Delivered from a slight crouching position, an uppercut is a short-range strike that curves upwards, usually towards the chin. It can result in an instant knockout if it strikes home and snaps the head back.